RACE CARS
UP CLOSE

★ **Andra Serlin Abramson** ★

STERLING

New York / London
www.sterlingpublishing.com/kids

STERLING and the distinctive Sterling logo are registered trademarks of
Sterling Publishing Co., Inc.

Library of Congress Cataloging-in-Publication Data

Abramson, Andra Serlin.
 Race cars up close / Andra Serlin Abramson.
    p. cm.
 ISBN 978-1-4027-5641-2
 1. Automobiles, Racing--Juvenile literature. I. Title.

TL236.A287 2008
796.72--dc22

                            2007048215

10 9 8 7 6 5 4 3 2 1

Published by Sterling Publishing Co., Inc.
387 Park Avenue South, New York, NY 10016
© 2008 by Sterling Publishing Co., Inc.
Distributed in Canada by Sterling Publishing
c/o Canadian Manda Group, 165 Dufferin Street
Toronto, Ontario, Canada M6K 3H6
Distributed in the United Kingdom by GMC Distribution Services
Castle Place, 166 High Street, Lewes, East Sussex, England BN7 1XU
Distributed in Australia by Capricorn Link (Australia) Pty. Ltd.
P.O. Box 704, Windsor, NSW 2756, Australia

Cover & interior design: T. Reitzle/Oxygen-Design

Jacket/Cover Photo Credits
Front cover top: © Nigel/Shutterstock
Front cover middle: Gilbert King
Front cover bottom left and bottom middle: © Donald Miralle/Getty Images
Front cover bottom right: © Mark Thompson/Getty Images
Back cover top: © John Thys/AFP/Getty Images
Back cover middle: Gilbert King
Back cover bottom: © Celso Diniz/Shutterstock
Inside front cover main: Gilbert King
Inside front cover top: © Jonathan Daniel/Getty Images
Inside front cover middle: © Jonathan Daniel/Getty Images
Inside front cover bottom: Gilbert King
Inside back cover main: Gilbert King
Inside back cover right: © Jason Smith/Getty Images for NASCAR
Inside back cover left: © Jonathan Daniel/Getty Images

Sterling ISBN 978-1-4027-5641-2

For information about custom editions, special sales, premium
and corporate purchases, please contact Sterling Special Sales
Department at 800-805-5489 or specialsales@sterlingpublishing.com.

Contents

Both race cars and racetracks have come a long way since the early days of auto racing. Today's automobile races combine the newest in automobile technology with human skills honed by years of practice to create a thrilling and often hair-raising racing event.

START YOUR ENGINES

EVERY WEEKEND, MILLIONS OF PEOPLE head to the track or turn on their televisions to watch auto racing. The thrill of watching cars zoom around the track at more than 200 miles (322 kilometers) per hour has made automobile racing one of the most popular sports in the world.

In June of 1949, 13,000 fans came to watch the first real NASCAR race. The race, held on a dirt track in Charlotte, North Carolina, had a purse of $2,000.

NASCAR Racing

NASCAR stands for the National Association for Stock Car Auto Racing. "Stock Cars" used to be cars that were the same "stock" as any other car of the same model found on the street. A racer could simply go to a car dealership, buy a car, and go stock racing. Today's racing cars, however, are far from what can be found in the dealer's stock. While all stock cars begin with one of three body types— the Dodge Intrepid, the Ford Taurus, or the Chevrolet Monte Carlo—racing teams that compete on a national level have supercharged nearly every part of their cars, trying to get an advantage over all the other teams.

Formula One Racing

Formula One—also known as F1 or Grand Prix racing—features open-cockpit cars (right photo). The first Formula One race was held in 1946. Today, Grand Prix races are held all over the world on both circuit courses and closed roads. Formula One racing is considered the world's most expensive sport, and the trials and tribulations of the racing teams are closely watched by fans in more than 200 countries.

Sponsorship

One of the most well-known aspects of auto racing is sponsorship—the advertisements splashed over every car and all around the racetracks. Some corporations spend an estimated $1 billion each year for the right to sponsor a racing team or advertise to racing fans. Since funding a racing team costs so much money—a team might spend as much as $1 million each season just on tires alone—these sponsorships are a necessary part of the auto racing business.

Just transporting a car from race to race can be an expensive proposition. Sponsorship helps the racing teams pay for some of these costs.

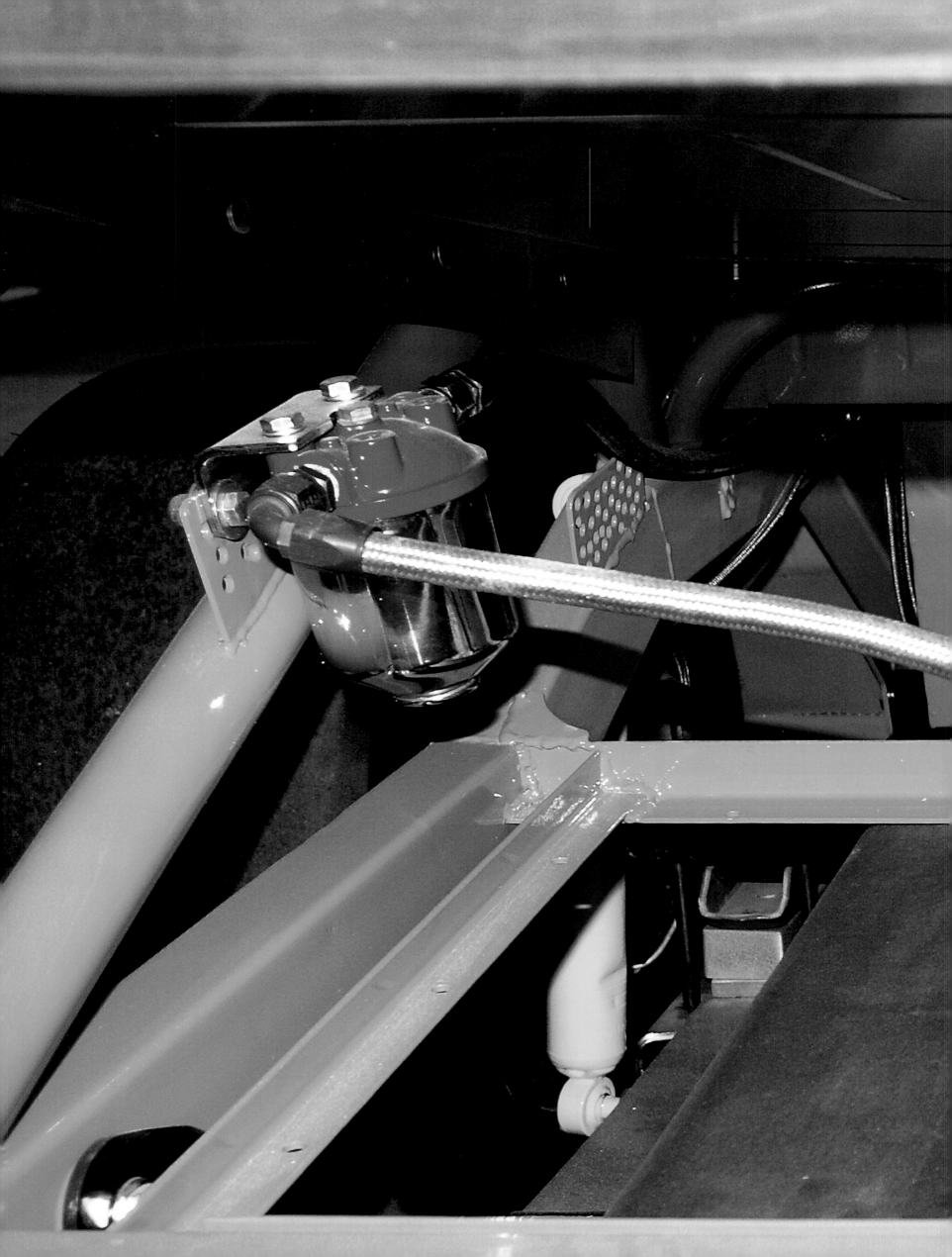

BUILDING A RACE CAR

EVEN THOUGH A NASCAR car starts out with the same body as a regular car, engineers make lots of adjustments to turn it into an efficient racing machine. In fact, only the hood of the car, the trunk lid, the roof, the front grille, and the bumpers are close to what you'd see on a regular passenger car, and even these are changed a bit to comply with NASCAR standards. Everything else is handmade specifically for each car by the racing team.

The headlights you see on NASCAR racing cars are just decals designed to make the cars look more like regular passenger cars.

From designing to molding, welding to sanding, virtually every piece of a race car is touched by the hand of a specially trained engineer.

Not Carbon Copies

The bodies of Formula One race cars are made from scratch out of composites of carbon fiber, which are expensive to manufacture and make the car very lightweight. Each Formula One car must weigh at least 1,334 pounds (605 kilograms), including the driver, fuel, and other equipment. The car itself is usually so light that ballast is added to meet the minimum requirement.

Once a car reaches the racetrack, the racing team works to make sure everything is as perfect as the day it left the garage.

The fuel tank in a stock car is called a fuel cell. It holds 22 gallons (83 liters) of gasoline and is specially mounted and cushioned to prevent ruptures, which could lead to explosions.

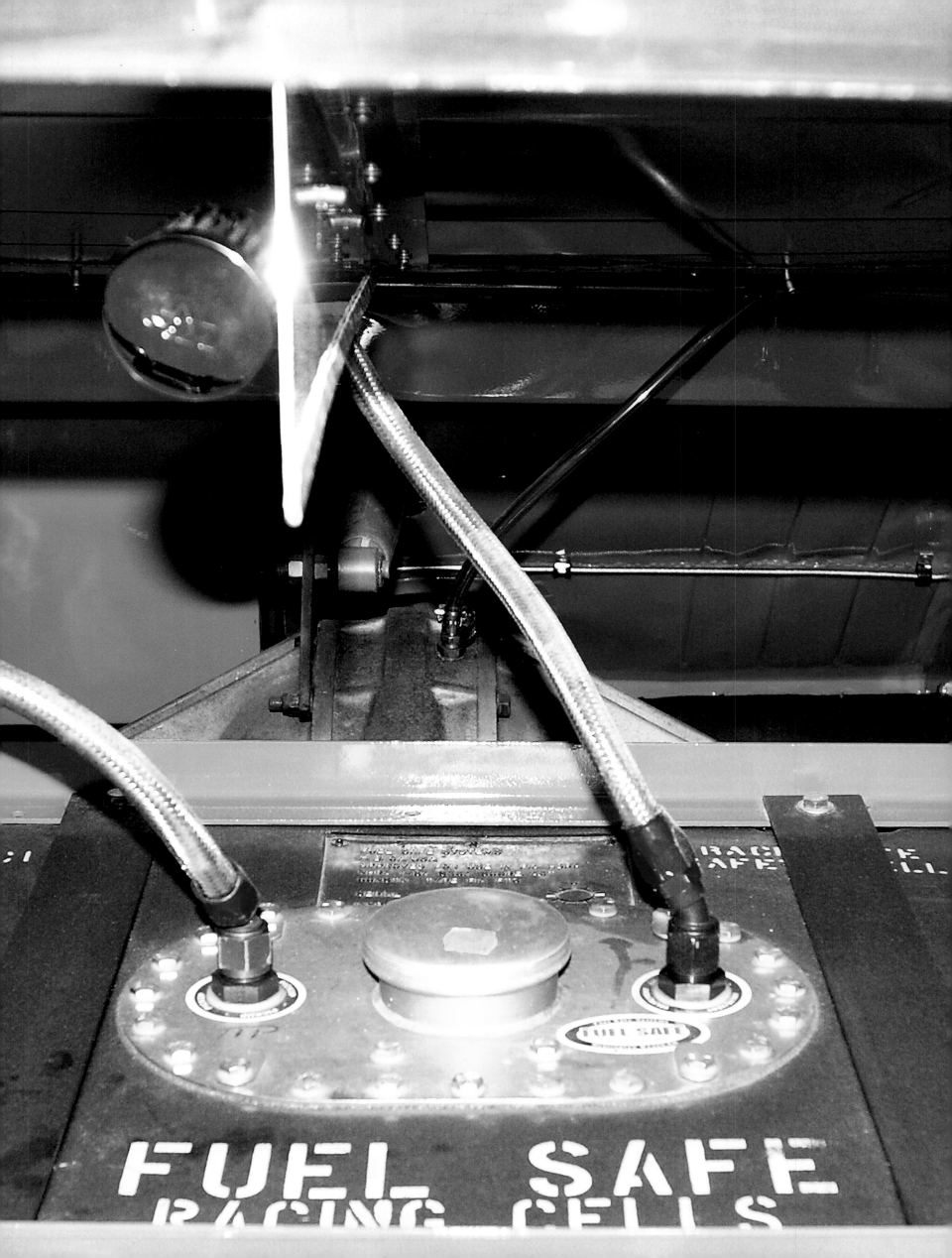

RACING SERIES

NASCAR RACES ARE DIVIDED into several different series, each geared toward drivers with different levels of talent. The highest-profile series is called the NASCAR NEXTEL Series. These are the races, such as the Daytona 500, that have the most famous drivers (including Jeff Gordon, Jimmie Johnson, and Dale Earnhardt Jr.) competing for pots worth millions of dollars. The Busch Series is considered a stepping-stone to the NEXTEL Series. It is a place where drivers can train with the hope of getting to the big leagues. Other famous series are the NASCAR Craftsman Truck Series and the Touring Division, where young drivers often get their start.

When Lowe's Motor Speedway in Charlotte, North Carolina, hosts the Coca-Cola 600, the 180,000 attendees temporarily make the Speedway the state's fourth-largest city.

Signing autographs, talking to fans, and doing interviews don't have anything to do with driving a race car, but they are important parts of a driver's job.

The NASCAR Craftsman Truck Series was started in 1995. Today, the series acts as a training ground for drivers looking to move to the Busch and NEXTEL Series.

The beginning of a NASCAR race is one of the most exciting parts, with each driver struggling to get even a few feet ahead of the other cars.

One hundred thousand NASCAR fans make a lot of noise, but not enough to drown out the noise of more than twenty high-powered racing engines.

Staging A Race

Racetracks must have all the facilities needed to keep a crowd of as many as 180,000 people safe and entertained (and fed!). From tickets to parking, food to restrooms, security to grounds crew, it takes thousands of people to run a racetrack. Preparation for a major race begins months and even years before the actual event takes place.

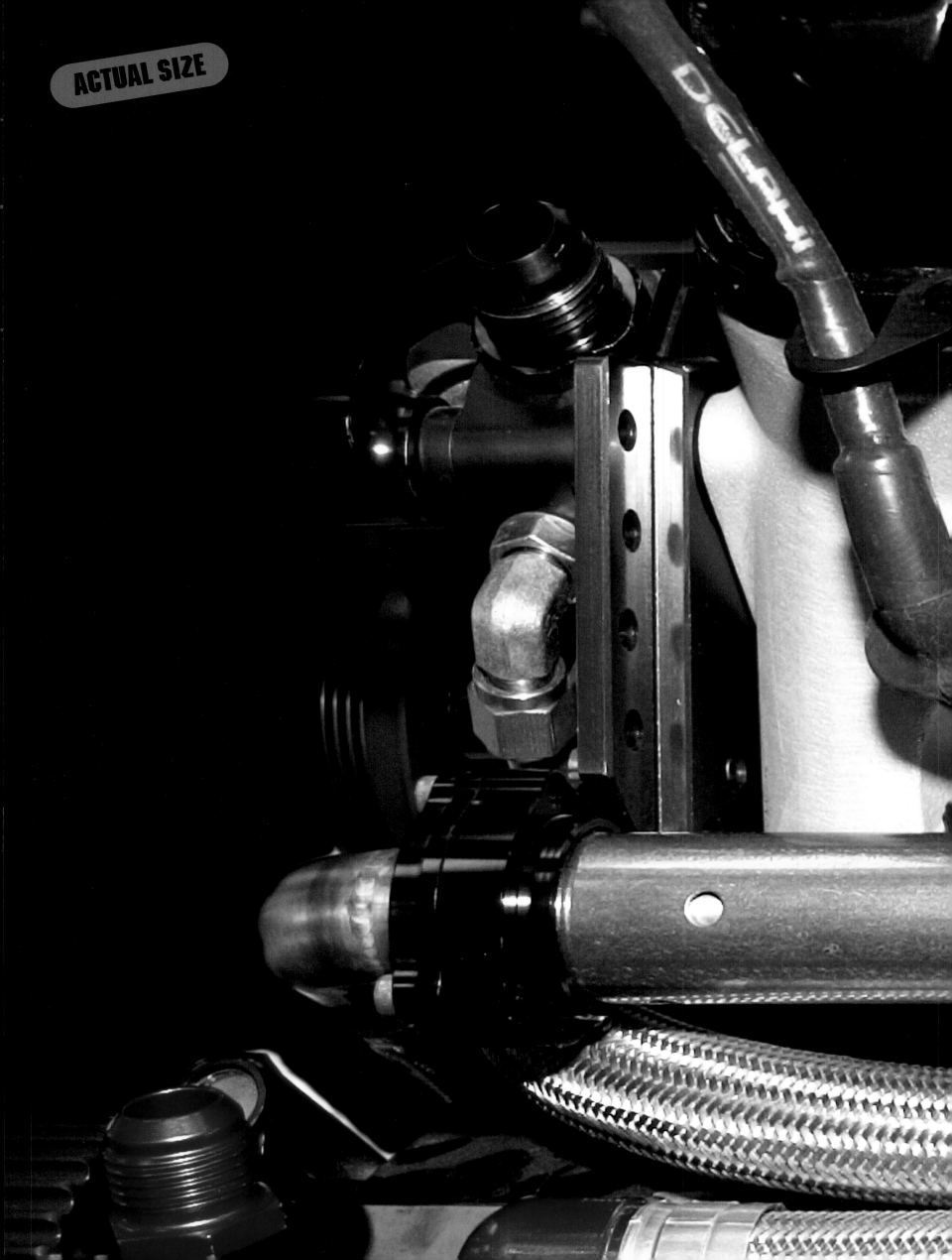

ACTUAL SIZE

With all of the care that goes into crafting a Formula One engine, it is no wonder that it is as beautiful as it is functional.

RACE CAR ENGINES

WHEN IT COMES TO A RACE CAR engine, bigger is definitely better—every piece of the engine is built for maximum endurance and power. Race car engines are hand-built specifically for each car and driver. Top stock car racers use one of three different kinds of engines—Ford, Dodge, or Chevrolet. Engines cost about $40,000 each, and every team has several on-hand for each race.

A race car's exhaust system exits through pipes that are installed on the right side of the car (see above), opposite the driver. This keeps the hot exhaust from making the interior of the car too warm.

Engine Power

Engine power is measured in horsepower. A normal passenger car averages about 200 horsepower. A high-powered race car engine, however, can produce about 750 horsepower for hours at a time. Another way to measure the power of an engine is through RPMs (revolutions per minute or the number of times a crankshaft turns per minute). A passenger car would probably break down if its engine ever hit 5,000 RPM. Race car engines can approach 8,900 RPM and maintain that rate for as long as needed.

RACING LIKE A PRO

· ·

DRIVING A RACE CAR is an exciting and often dangerous career. Between practices, races, meetings with sponsors, and special appearances, a driver's schedule can be packed. And then, during a three- or four-hour-long race, a driver must stay focused every minute, searching for ways to help his or her car perform better, reduce the risk of an accident, and make up a few seconds of time.

There is no time for daydreaming when you are behind the wheel of a race car going 200 miles (322 kilometers) per hour!

Posing for photos is just one of the jobs of a professional race car driver. Race car drivers work just as hard off the track as they do on it.

Driver = Athlete

While it may seem like anyone with a driver's license could be a race car driver, the reality is that today's race car drivers need to be in tip-top shape, just like the competitors in any other sport. In order to be successful, race car drivers need lightning-fast reflexes to help them steer away from accidents that might happen just a few feet ahead of them. They also need good coordination to smoothly switch gears, step on the brake, or rev up the accelerator. Race car drivers also need excellent upper-body strength to steer the car around turns at such great speeds!

Practice, Practice, and More Practice

In car racing—just like in every other sport—practice is essential. Before a race, each racing team takes turns having the track all to itself for a short period of time. As the driver takes the car around for practice laps, he or she talks with his or her team members over the radio, letting them know exactly what is happening with the car. This is the team's only chance to make sure the car is running perfectly after its trip to the track.

Concentration is key for a professional race car driver, who must be able to keep his or her mind on the race every second.

Race cars don't have side view mirrors, so drivers rely on *spotters* to let them know (over a radio) if there is enough room to pass a car. The spotter sits high above the track—with a full view of all of the action—and acts as the driver's second set of eyes.

The way a driver works with and communicates with his or her racing team can mean the difference between victory and defeat.

A rollbar is designed to protect the driver in the event of a crash that causes the car to flip over.

Although officials believe that restrictor plates make racing safer, some drivers believe the opposite. They argue that because the cars all have the same maximum speed, packs of cars form, resulting in multi-car pile-ups.

Racing teams keep several different engines on hand in case one isn't functioning as well as it should and needs to be replaced.

Restrictor Plates

The addition of a restrictor plate to an engine is one of the most controversial issues in car racing. A *carburetor restrictor plate* is a metal plate with four holes drilled into it that limits the amount of horsepower a car can produce. For example, a race car without a restrictor plate can reach about 210 miles (338 kilometers) per hour. However, a race car with a restrictor plate usually only goes between 190 and 200 miles (306 and 322 kilometers) per hour. A restrictor plate is required for some races, such as the Daytona 500.

ACTUAL SIZE

No "Mechanics" Needed

It might seem like a racing team would need several mechanics to keep the race car running at its best. Some racing teams do employ general mechanics, but usually there are specialists to take care of every conceivable part of the car. For example, there are engine builders who build the engine from scratch. There are also suspension specialists, tire specialists, parts specialists, not to mention engine specialists. The job of the engine specialist is to take care of the engine after it gets to the racetrack.

Thousands of adjustments are made by hand to each and every race car—both in the garage and at the track—to keep them working at peak performance.

Because even the smallest tweaks can make the difference between winning and losing, NASCAR race car engines are considered top secret and are rarely allowed to be photographed.

STAYING SAFE

EVERY PART OF A NASCAR racing car is designed to help a driver be able to walk away from an accident. There is a *five-point harness restraint* (seatbelt) that features two straps that come down over the driver's shoulders, two straps that come around the waist, and one that comes up between the legs. This type of seatbelt keeps the driver in his or her seat no matter how many times the car might turn over in an accident.

Stock cars don't have glass windows or windshields. During an accident, the glass could shatter, injuring the driver. Instead, the front and rear windshields are made of a material called Lexan, which is a shatterproof plastic. Stock cars also feature rubber gas tanks, which are less likely to explode on impact.

Helmets, gloves, jumpsuits, and fire-retardant long underwear are all must-haves for a driver in a professional automobile race.

Racing Uniforms

A race car driver wears a jumpsuit that is fire-resistant and covers the driver from neck to ankle. Also worn are fire-retardant long underwear, gloves, and insulated boots that protect his or her feet from the intense heat of the floorboards and pedals. Finally, a full-face helmet protects the driver's head in the event of a crash.

Reed Sorenson's orange jumpsuit is designed to protect him in the event of a crash.

The cockpit of a Formula One race car (above) is designed to form a protective shell—called a *survival cell*—around the driver in case of an accident. The survival cell includes the driver's seat, which is made to fit a driver's exact dimensions.

Besides money, the winning driver takes home a trophy to commemorate his or her win. Here, Carl Edwards, driver of the #99 Office Depot Ford, celebrates in Victory Lane after winning the NASCAR NEXTEL Series Sharpie 500 at Bristol Motor Speedway in Bristol, Tennessee.

After winning a race, the entire racing team has the chance to celebrate in Victory Lane.

VICTORY LANE

FOR A DRIVER, THE TEAM OWNER, and all the people who work hard to make the car the best it can be, the goal is to get to NASCAR's Victory Lane or Formula One's Winner's Circle. Despite the name, Victory Lane isn't really a road. It's actually a fenced-in area where a driver and his or her crew go to celebrate after winning a race. Victory Lane is packed with people congratulating the driver, including the driver's family, journalists, photographers, track officials, and sponsor representatives.

The cockpit of a race car doesn't much look like the cockpit of a passenger car. It is designed to give the driver total control of every aspect of his or her vehicle.

IN THE DRIVER'S SEAT

GETTING BEHIND THE WHEEL of a high-speed stock car is a rush only a handful of people ever get to experience. If you are lucky enough to climb into one of these vehicles, the first thing you might notice is that the doors don't open. Instead, the driver climbs into the cockpit through the window. The second thing you might notice is that there is no steering wheel—it needs to be attached once you are inside the car. This makes it easier for the driver to enter and exit the car.

Tony Stewart, driver of the #18 Goody's Cool Orange Chevrolet, gets out of his car during qualifying for the NASCAR Busch Series O'Reilly Challenge at Texas Motor Speedway in Fort Worth, Texas.

Whether taking a test run or driving in a high-profile race, a driver must communicate with his or her team every detail of how the car is working so that adjustments can be made.

Fun with a Purpose

Everything inside a race car has a purpose. There are no frills, no extras, nothing that is there just for comfort. A race car needs to be light to be fast, so it is stripped down to the bare essentials. Only the basic mechanisms and the safety equipment remain. Even the side window glass has been removed (and replaced with netting) to make the car lighter and to protect the driver in the event of a crash.

Taking Home the Winnings

The amount of money a driver receives at the end of a race is called the race *purse*. The amount offered in a purse varies from race to race and track to track. Some purses are huge—more than a million dollars for the winner of the Daytona 500, for example. But even the driver who finishes last in a NASCAR race still makes money for his or her efforts.

After crossing the finish line, drivers have a chance to take a victory lap around the track, often waving the checkered flag that marked their win.

While a driver may make more than a million dollars per race, he or she generally takes home only around 50 percent of the money won. The rest goes to the team owner, who has to pay the salaries of the rest of team and the costs of maintaining the car.

Danica Patrick is one of a few women professional race car drivers. In 2005, Danica was named Rookie of the Year for both the Indianapolis 500 and the IndyCar Series season.

Meet the Women Who Win

The first woman to race in a NASCAR Cup series was Janet Guthrie in the mid-1970s. Other women have followed in her footsteps including Kelly Sutton, a regular NASCAR Craftsman Truck Series driver. Danica Patrick finished 7th in the overall IndyCar Racing standings in 2007.

RACETRACKS

A view of Martinsville Speedway in Martinsville, Virgina, at the NASCAR NEXTEL Series Subway 500.

WHEN RACE DAY ARRIVES, thousands of people head to the racetrack to watch their favorite drivers compete. Most racetracks are oval in shape, but each has its own share of challenges for the drivers. Whether flat or *high-banked* (having a racing surface that is steeply sloped), with a smooth surface or rough, each track is designed to provide a unique racing experience for drivers and fans alike.

The steep slope on some race-tracks makes driving a challenge.

The safety fence restraints seen here are designed to keep spectators safe in the event of a crash.

Soft Walls

All racetracks have concrete retaining walls designed to keep out-of-control cars inside the racing area and away from spectators. Some racetracks have an additional "soft" wall made of energy-absorbing crushable material that lessens the force of the impact with the retaining wall.

Track workers repair the wall following a crash during the NASCAR Busch Series Camping World 300 at Auto Club Speedway in Fontana, California.

Formula One Circuits

Formula One races are held on tracks called *circuits*. There is no such thing as a typical circuit, although most tracks have a stretch of straight road where the starting grid and pit lane are located. Formula One also has street circuits in which the cars race on regular (but closed to traffic!) streets. The two street circuits that run every year take place in Monaco (in May) and Melbourne, Australia (in March)—both are huge, multi-day events that attract tens of thousands of spectators.

Most Formula One circuits run in a clockwise direction. Those that run counterclockwise, and therefore have many left-turn corners, can cause neck problems for drivers because the turns pull the drivers' heads in the opposite direction that they're used to.

Formula One racetracks, like the Circuit of SPA-Francorchamps in Belgium, look very different from those used in NASCAR races.

The cars pull away at the start of the Monaco Formula One Grand Prix at the Monte Carlo Circuit on May 28, 2006, in Monte Carlo, Monaco.

With no treads on their tires, race cars wouldn't fare very well on the often unpredictable roads found outside a racetrack.

MOOG

CHASSIS PARTS

CLEVITE

Each racing team needs to have dozens of tires on hand for each race.

RACING WHEELS

The tires on a Formula One race car are outside the body of the car, where the driver can see them.

LIKE THE WHEELS ON A REGULAR CAR, the wheels on a race car are black and round. However, the similarities end there. Unlike regular tires, which rely on their treads to give them traction, NASCAR race car wheels have no treads at all. Instead, these wheels are sticky to the touch, giving them a better grip on the racetrack surface. Also, while the tires on a regular car might last as long as 50,000 miles (80,467 kilometers) before needing to be replaced, race car tires need to be changed, on average, every 75 to 100 miles (121 to 161 kilometers).

Formula One car tires have four large circumferential grooves that are designed to limit the cornering speed of the cars. Tires are so important to the success of a race car that many drivers consider them the most vital element on the car. Today, all Formula One tires come from one supplier, which helps eliminate some of the differences between cars.

A crew member tightens the allen bolts on a wheel hub during a NASCAR NEXTEL Series.

ACTUAL SIZE

The Dashboard

To start a race car, the driver just flips a switch on the dashboard and presses the starter button. No key is needed. Other switches turn on a fan to cool the rear brakes, turn on the radiator fan, and switch on a blower to bring fresh air to the driver. Surprisingly, a race car has no speedometer to tell the driver how fast he or she is going. Instead, the driver monitors gauges that measure oil pressure, oil temperature, and water temperature, indicating how well the engine is running.

A NASCAR driver flips a switch to turn on the engine in his or her car.

The driver's seat in a race car is designed to fit his or her body like a glove. The seat is molded to fit around the driver's ribs and wrap around his or her shoulders. This gives the driver better support in a crash by spreading the impact over the entire body instead of just one area.

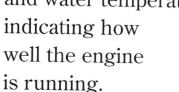

The cockpit controls of a Formula One race car are designed to put everything the driver needs right at his or her fingertips.

ACTUAL SIZE

Race car tires are filled with nitrogen, not regular air. This is because the moisture found in air can expand when it gets hot, causing a change in tire pressure. Since even a small change in tire pressure will affect the handling of a high-tech race car, using nitrogen—which does not expand when heated—can make the car more stable at high speeds.

New tires are called sticker tires *because they still have the manufacturer's sticker on them.* Scuffs *are tires that have been used for a lap or two during practice.*

The Inner Liner

On any racetrack that is longer than one mile, NASCAR racing rules require each tire to have an *inner liner.* An inner liner is basically a second tire mounted on the wheel inside the regular tire. This inner wheel acts as a safety precaution, because if the outer tire blows out during a race, the inner liner tire allows the driver to safely control the car until he or she can get back to the pit for a tire change.

When a tire blows, it really blows, making the inner liner an important safety measure.

FLAGGED DOWN

ONCE A RACE GETS STARTED, a driver needs to keep his or her eyes both on the road and on the flag waver who is perched high above the racetrack at the start/finish point. The flag waver is in constant contact with the race control tower, where all decisions about race operations are made.

Race conditions are closely monitored by the control tower and relayed to the flag waver.

The scoring team keeps track of each car in a race to ensure that it completes all of the necessary laps. Each car's progress is recorded four different ways—from marking down each lap by hand to using an electronic monitor on each car to record its position—to make sure that all races are honest and complete.